John R. Sweney

Gospel Hosannas

A choice collection of hymns and tunes for use in evangelistic,

brotherhood and mission meetings, Sunday-school

John R. Sweney

Gospel Hosannas
A choice collection of hymns and tunes for use in evangelistic, brotherhood and mission meetings, Sunday-school

ISBN/EAN: 9783337083618

Printed in Europe, USA, Canada, Australia, Japan

Cover: Foto ©Lupo / pixelio.de

More available books at **www.hansebooks.com**

SHAPED NOTE.

Gospel Hosannas

A CHOICE COLLECTION OF

Hymns and Tunes for use in Evangelistic, Brotherhood and Mission Meetings, Sunday=school, Etc.

COMPILED BY

JOHN R. SWENEY and J. HOWARD ENTWISLE

PHILADELPHIA

THE UNION PRESS	JOHN J. HOOD
1816 Chestnut Street	1024 Arch Street

COPYRIGHT, 1898, BY THE AMERICAN SUNDAY-SCHOOL UNION AND JOHN J. HOOD

Price, $10.00 per 100, express not prepaid: if by mail, add 2 cents per copy for postage.

GOSPEL HOSANNAS.

1. JESUS GUIDES ME ALL THE WAY.

W. J. S.
Rev. W. J. Stuart, A. M.

1. Out of shad-ow in-to light, Out of blind-ness in-to sight; Out of darkness in-to day,
2. Out of sor-row in-to joy, Praise his name! 'tis sweet employ Ev-er to my Lord to pray;
3. Out of sin-ning in-to grace, At his feet I find my place; Ev-er with my Lord to stay,
4. Ev-er with him I'll a-bide, Spot-less, by his riv-en side; Here I'll live, I'll nev-er stray,
5. Out of life in-to the tomb, By his side there is no gloom; From the throne there comes a ray,

CHORUS.
Jesus guides me all the way. Je-sus, Je-sus guides me, Guides me all the way; Out of darkness in-to day, Jesus guides me all the way.

Copyright, 1896, by Jno. R. Sweney.

6 Out of death to endless life,
Up from all the sin and strife;
Clothed upon with white array,
Jesus guides me all the way.

7 Up before the throne of gold,
I shall know a joy untold;
With the blood-washed I will say,
Jesus guides me all the way.

JOIN, YE SONS OF MEN.

"The chiefest among ten thousand; yea, he is the altogether lovely."—Solomon's Song.

W. S. M.   W. S. MARTIN.

1. Je-sus is the Al-to-geth-er Love-ly, Yea, he is the fair-est of the fair; Oh, who is there in heav'n a-bove be-side him, Who on earth can with my Lord com-pare?
2. Je-sus is the Al-to-geth-er Love-ly, Sweet-er than the hon-ey is his word: 'Tis filled with precious prom-is-es of mer-cy For the soul who puts his trust in God.
3. Je-sus is the Al-to-geth-er Love-ly, O-pen now thy heart to him a-lone, For in his death and glo-rious res-ur-rec-tion He to us the grace of God hath shown.

D.S.—See him on the cross for man's sal-va-tion, Suff-'ring death and bear-ing sin and shame.

CHORUS.

Join, ye sons of men, in ad-o-ra-tion, Give to him the hon-or due his name;

Copyright, 1889, by John J. Hood.

JESUS LEADS.

"And when he putteth forth his own sheep, he goeth before them, and the sheep follow him, for they know his voice."—John x : 4.

JOHN R. CLEMENTS.　　　　　　　　　　　　　　　　　　　　　JNO. R. SWENEY.

Andante

1. Like a shep-herd, ten-der, true, Je- sus leads,...... Je - sus leads,......
2. All a - long life's rugged road Je- sus leads,...... Je - sus leads,......
3. Thro' the sun - lit ways of life Je- sus leads,...... Je - sus leads,......

Je - sus leads,　　　Je - sus leads,

Dai- ly finds us pastures new, Je- sus leads,...... Je - sus leads ;
Till we reach yon blest a - bode, Je- sus leads,...... Je - sus leads ;
Thro' the warrings and the strife, Je- sus leads,...... Je - sus leads ;

Je - sus leads,　　　Je - sus leads ;

If thick mists... are o'er the way,... Or the flock... 'mid danger feeds,
All the way,.... be-fore, he's trod, And he now.... the flock precedes,
When we reach the Jordan's tide, Where life's bound-'ry-line re-cedes,

If thick mists are o'er the way, Or the flock 'mid danger feeds,

rit............

He will watch them lest they stray, Je- sus leads,...... Je - sus leads.
Safe in - to the fold of God Je- sus leads,...... Je - sus leads.
He will spread the waves a - side, Je- sus leads,...... Je - sus leads.

Je - sus leads,

Copyright, 1893, by Jno. R. Sweney.

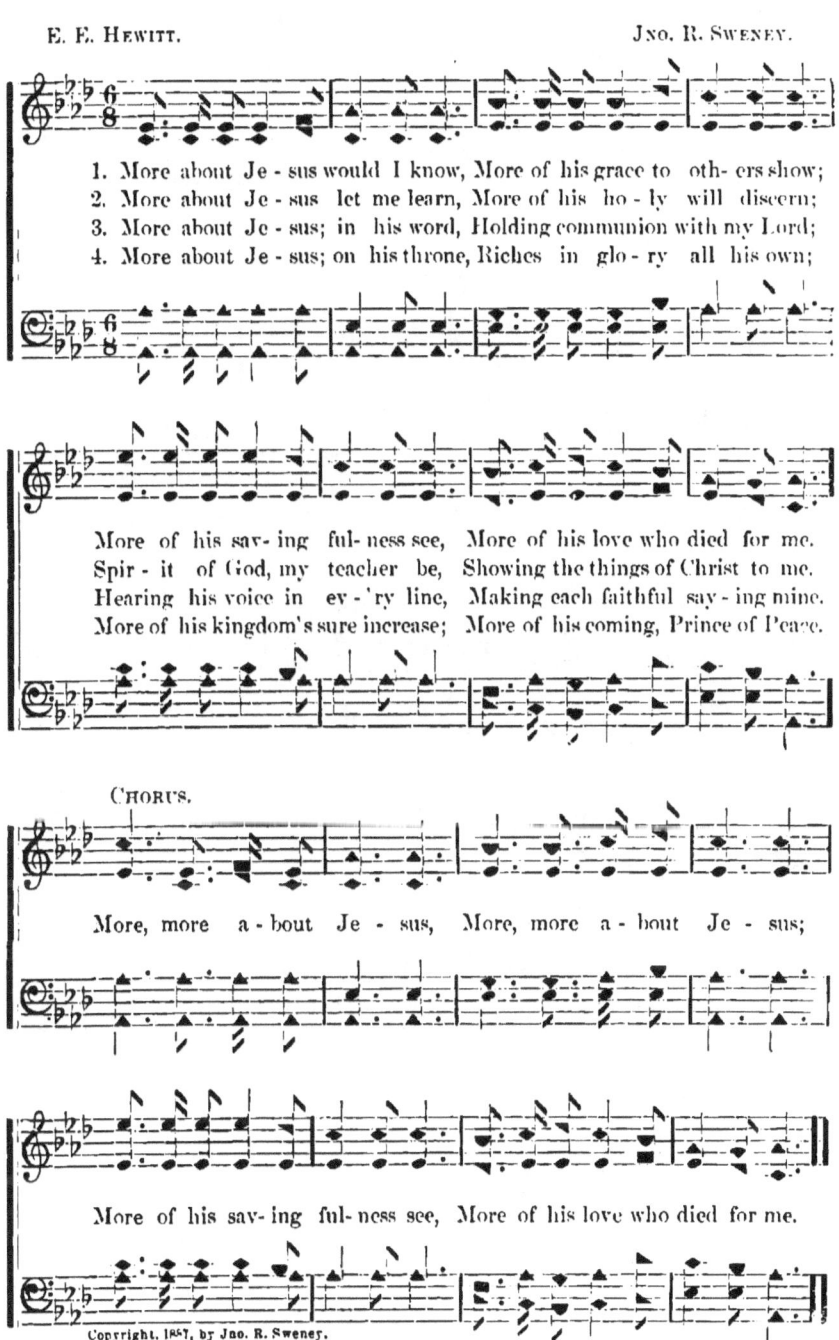

I WILL SAY "YES" TO JESUS.—CONCLUDED.

With outstretch'd hands my Saviour stands, And beckons the wand'rer to come;
the wand'rer to come;
Without de-lay I'll now o-bey, And he will welcome me home..........
will welcome me home.

11   THE GOLDEN KEY.
"Prayer is the key to unlock the door, and the bolt to shut in the night."
JNO. R. SWENEY.

1. Prayer is the key For the bending knee To open the morn's first hours,
2. Not a soul so sad, Nor a heart so glad, When cometh the shades of night,
3. Take the golden key In your hand and see, As the night tide drifts away,

See the incense rise To the star-ry skies, Like perfume from the flow'rs.
But the daybreak song Will the joy prolong, And some darkness turn to light.
How its blessed hold Is a crown of gold, Thro' the weary hours of day.

Copyright, 1875, by John J. Hood.

4 When the shadows fall,
  And the vesper call
Is sobbing its low refrain,
  'Tis a garland sweet
  To the toil-dent feet,
And an antidote for pain.

5 Soon the year's dark door
  Shall be shut no more:
Life's tears shall be wiped away,
  As the pearl gates swing,
  And the gold harps ring,
And the sun unsheathes for aye.

15. THE CALL TO ARMS.

J. H. E.
J. Howard Entwisle.

1. There's a call for soldiers on the field of bat-tle, There's a fight to win o'er Satan's host arrayed; Then gird your ar-mor on, Go forth to fight the wrong, Be not a-fraid, for Je-sus leads the way.
2. There's a call for soldiers on the field of bat-tle, There is earnest need for workers true and brave; Tho' fierce the conflict be, Tho' strong the foemen be, Press firmly on, the cause of Christ to save.
3. Be-hold! our Captain lead-eth on to vic-to-ry. And Satan's horde is scattered far and near; Then shout the bat-tle-cry, With ban-ners waving high, The God of bat-tle leads us, do not fear.

D.C.—Then gird your ar-mor on, go forth to fight the wrong, Be not dismayed, tho' fierce the conflict be; Then on to vic-to-ry! Then on to vic-to-ry! "For Je-sus on-ly" let the watchword be.

CHORUS.

1, 2.—See the hosts of sin advanc-ing, Sa-tan is lead-ing on, Then
3.—See the hosts of sin retreat-ing, Sa-tan is lead-ing on, Then
on for Je-sus! on for Je-sus! Ev-er singing the victor's song.

Copyright, 1897, by John J. Hood.

4 My yoke is easy,—burden light,
   Since Christ the Lord is mine!
   Each day my pathway seems more bright,
   Since Christ the Lord is mine!

5 In him I have each need supplied,
   Since Christ the Lord is mine!
   In him my soul is satisfied,
   Since Christ the Lord is mine!

CROSSING ONE BY ONE.—CONCLUDED.

ev - er to a - bide,—We shall cross the mys-tic riv - er, one by one.

21   THE LIFE ON WINGS.

Mrs. FRANK A. BRECK. JNO. R. SWENEY.

1. My soul, stay not in shadows, Where the mist of sorrow clings; There is
2. On wings of faith mount upward, Far be-yond all earthly things; There is
3. There's triumph in all tr - ial, 'Tis the peace that Jesus brings; O'er the

joy for the heart bidding shadows depart, There is joy for the life on wings.
peace that will last till thy journey is past, There is joy for the life on wings.
faith-mounted soul sorrow hath no control, There is joy for the life on wings.

CHORUS.

Mount up, my soul, with glad-ness, Where the sun-shine cheers and warms;

The life on wings is the life that sings, Then soar a-bove the storms.

Copyright, 1898, by Jno. R. Sweney.

LEND A HAND.—CONCLUDED.

25. NEARER, MY GOD, TO THEE!

Mrs. Sarah F. Adams.   Rev. S. G. Neil.

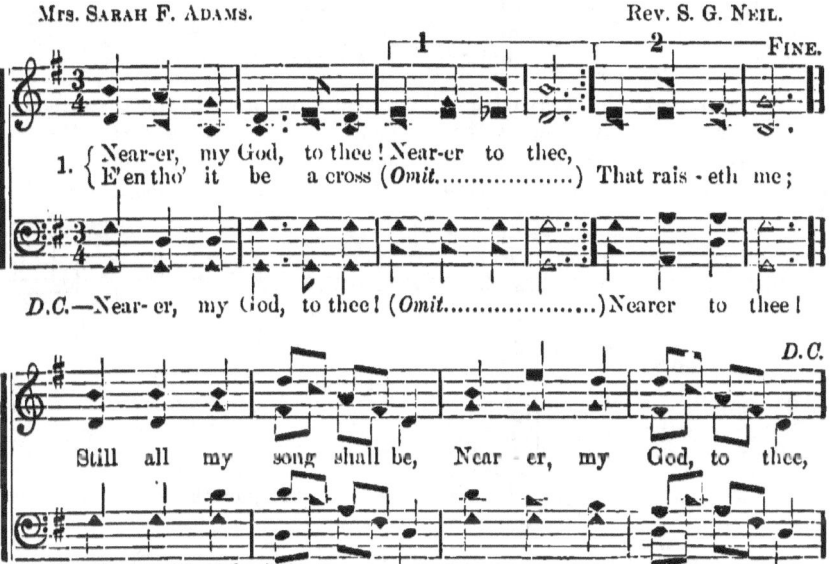

2 Though like the wanderer,
   The sun gone down,
Darkness be over me,
   My rest a stone,
Yet in my dreams I'd be
Nearer, my God, to thee,
   Nearer to thee!

3 There let the way appear,
   Steps unto heaven;
All that thou sendest me,
   In mercy given,
Angels to beckon me
Nearer, my God, to thee,
   Nearer, to thee!

4 Then, with my waking thoughts
   Bright with thy praise,
Out of my stony griefs
   Bethel I'll raise;
So by my woes to be
Nearer, my God, to thee,
   Nearer to thee!

5 Or if, on joyful wing,
   Cleaving the sky,
Sun, moon, and stars forgot,
   Upward I fly,
Still all my song shall be,
Nearer, my God, to thee,
   Nearer to thee!

Gospel Hosannas—D   This hymn is also sung to the tune "Bethany."

31 STEP BY STEP.

ADA BLENKHORN.   J. HOWARD ENTWISLE.

1. Where'er he leads us we can go, Step by step, step by step;
2. As Jesus liv'd, so may we live, Step by step, step by step;
3. His works of love we all can do, Step by step, step by step;

The bless-ed way to oth-ers show, Walk-ing step by step.
And to his name the glo-ry give, Walk-ing step by step.
And be to his ex-am-ple true, Walk-ing step by step.

CHORUS.
Step, step, step by step, While walking thus we can-not stray;
He'll lead us safe-ly in his way, Walk-ing step by step.

Copyright, 1898, by John J. Hood.

4 The way to heav'n we may pursue,
   Step by step, step by step;
   And keep the cross and crown in view,
   Walking step by step.

5 The life divine we can attain,
   Step by step, step by step;
   And rise at last with him to reign,
   Walking step by step.

REDEEMED THRO' THE BLOOD.—CONCLUDED.

I am ful-ly sat-isfied, For I know thro' his blood I'm redeemed.
I am ful-ly,

33 WASH ME IN THY BLOOD.

E. E. Hewitt. Jno. R. Sweney.

1. O Lord, thy mighty grace impart, Wash me in thy blood; Take full pos-
2. From outward fault, from se-cret sin, Wash me in thy blood; Let now thy
3. Ar-ray my soul in robes divine, Wash me in thy blood; The garments
4. Un-til that happy day shall break, Wash me in thy blood; When in thy

CHORUS.

session of my heart, Wash me in thy blood. Saviour, make me all thine own,
Spir-it rule within, Wash me in thy blood.
of sal-vation mine, Wash me in thy blood.
likeness I awake, Wash me in thy blood.

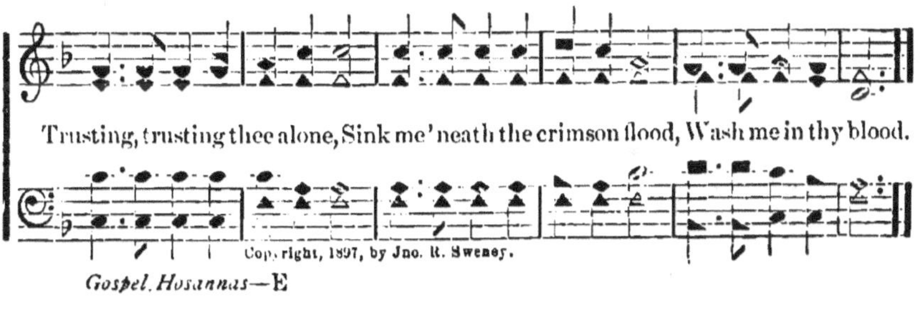

Trusting, trusting thee alone, Sink me 'neath the crimson flood, Wash me in thy blood.

Copyright, 1897, by Jno. R. Sweney.

Gospel Hosannas—E

I'LL GO WHERE YOU WANT ME TO GO.

Mary Brown. Andante.   Carrie E. Rounsefell.

1. It may not be on the mountain's height, Or o-ver the storm-y sea;
2. Per-haps to-day there are loving words Which Jesus would have me speak—
3. There's surely somewhere a low-ly place, In earth's harvest fields so wide—

It may not be at the bat-tle's front My Lord will have need of me;
There may be now in the paths of sin Some wand'rer whom I should seek—
Where I may la-bor thro' life's short day For Je-sus the cru-ci-fied—

But, if by a still, small voice he calls To paths that I do not know,
O Sav-iour, if thou wilt be my guide, Tho' dark and rugged the way,
So trust-ing my all to thy ten-der care, And know-ing thou lovest me,

I'll answer, dear Lord, with my hand in thine, I'll go where you want me to go.
My voice shall echo thy mes-sage sweet, I'll say what you want me to say.
I'll do thy will with a heart sin-cere, I'll be what you want me to be.

Refrain.

I'll go where you want me to go, dear Lord, Over mountain, or plain, or sea;

Copyright, 1894, by C. E. Rounsefell, By per.

I'LL GO WHERE YOU, etc.—CONCLUDED.

I'll say what you want me to say, dear Lord, I'll be what you want me to be.

37 DON'T YOU KNOW HE CARES?

Like Elijah, when he sat under the Juniper tree and prayed for the Lord to take his life, how often we in hours of trouble, sit under our Juniper tree of sorrow alone and cry out, "I am passing through the waters and 'Nobody Cares.'"

Rev. JOHNSON OATMAN, Jr.   J. HOWARD ENTWISLE.

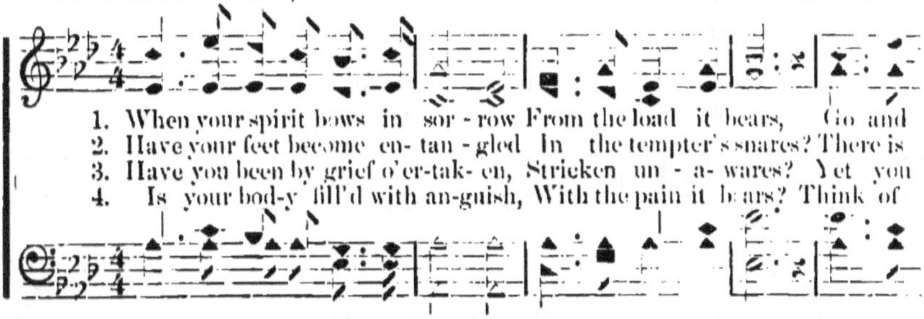

1. When your spirit bows in sor-row From the load it bears, Go and tell your heart to Jesus,—Don't you know he cares?
2. Have your feet become en-tan-gled In the tempter's snares? There is One who died to save you, Don't you know he cares?
3. Have you been by grief o'er-tak-en, Stricken un-a-wares? Yet you will not be for-sak-en, Don't you know he cares?
4. Is your bod-y fill'd with an-guish, With the pain it bears? Think of how the Saviour suffered—Don't you know he cares?

FINE. CHORUS.

Yes, there is One who shares your burdens, Ev'ry sorrow shares; Go and tell it all to Je-sus,—

D.S.—Don't you know he cares?

5 Loss of friends and loss of fortune—
  Life a dark look wears;
  Yet the Saviour still is with you,
  Don't you know he cares?

6 So amid life's cares and struggles,
  Blending songs with prayers—
  Always put your trust in Jesus,
  Don't you know he cares?

Copyright, 1897, by John J. Hood.

5 Will you have this blessing that Jesus bestows,
A free, full salvation—as ev'ry one knows?
Oh, sinner, poor sinner, to Calvary flee,
The blood of my Saviour was shed there for thee.

6 There is no one like Jesus, can cheer me to-day, [away,
His love and his kindness can ne'er fade
In winter, in summer, in sunshine and rain, [same.
His love and affection are always the

OUT BEYOND THE BREAKERS.

T. E. T. Rev. T. E. Terry.

1. There is a dan-ger line on the sea of life, It is mark'd by the
2. When the Is-ra-el of God came from Egypt land, They were stopp'd by the
3. Are you in the breakers, brother, and roughly toss'd, Is your soul in dis-

roar and the spray and the strife; There to lure our souls Satan does his best,
sea and the Jordan's stormy strand, Tho' they fear'd the waves with their foamy crests,
tress, have you peace and comfort lost? Let the shore-line go, pull a-way and trust,

CHORUS.

But out beyond the breakers there is rest, sweet rest. Out be-yond the
They knew that on the Canaan side was rest, sweet rest.
Get out be-yond the breakers, there is rest, sweet rest.

breakers as they dash and roll, Out beyond the breakers there is safety for the soul,

Out, launch out, 'till the storms are past, Out beyond the breakers we'll be safe at the last.

Copyright, 1898, by Jno. R. Sweney.

ELLEN DARE.   JNO. R. SWENEY.

1. Send out the sunlight, the sunlight of cheer, Shine on earth's sadness till it disap-
2. Send out the sunlight in letter and word; Speak it and think it till hearts are all
3. Send out the sunlight each hour and day, Crown all the years with its luminous
4. Send out the sunlight that speaks in a smile, Often it shortens the long, weary

pears—Souls are in waiting this message to hear, Send out the sunlight of love.
stirr'd—Hearts that are hungry for pray'rs still unheard, Send out the sunlight of love.
ray, Nourish the seeds that are sown on the way, Send out the sunlight of love.
mile, Often the burdens seem light for awhile, Send out the sunlight of love.

CHORUS.

Send out the sunlight of love,......... Send out the sunlight of love,.........
    the sunlight of love,   the sunlight of love,

Send out the sunlight, Send out the sunlight, Send out the sunlight of love.
                                                                        the sunlight of love.

Copyright, 1892, by Jno. R. Sweney.

5 Send out the sunlight, as free as the air!
Blessings will follow with none to com-
   pare,   [spair!
Blessings of peace, that will rise from de-
   Send out the sunlight of love.

6 Send out the sunlight, you have it in you!
Clouds may obscure it just now from your
   view;   [true,
Pray for its presence! your prayer will come
   Send out the sunlight of love.

50. NEVER SAY "NO" TO JESUS.

Rev. JOHNSON OATMAN, Jr.
Slow with expression.
J. HOWARD ENTWISLE.

1. In the fight against sin, If a crown you would win, Never say "no" to Je-sus; When his or-ders you hear, Move ahead, nev-er fear, Nev-er say "no" to Je-sus.
2. When he bids you to speak To a soul that is weak, Never say "no" to Je-sus; If he says, "lend a hand, That your brother may stand," Nev-er say "no" to Je-sus.
3. If he wants you to walk, If he wants you to talk, Never say "no" to Je-sus; If he bids you to stay, If he bids you to pray, Nev-er say "no" to Je-sus.

CHORUS.

No! no! nev-er say "no," Never say "no" to Je-sus; Oh, be faith-ful and true, What he tells you to do, Never say "no" to Jesus.

Copyright, 1898, by John J. Hood.

4 If he calls you to go
Where the deep waters flow,
Never say "no" to Jesus;
If he calls you to make
Sacrifice for his sake,
Never say "no" to Jesus.

5 If he calls you to give
All to him while you live,
Never say "no" to Jesus;
For at last, by and by,
He will call you on high,
Never say "no" to Jesus.

56. THOUGH YOUR SINS BE AS SCARLET.

"Though your sins be as scarlet, they shall be as white as snow."—Isaiah i. 18.

Fanny J. Crosby.   W. H. Doane. By per.

Copyright, 1887, by W. H. Doane.

OUR STRENGTH AND SHIELD.—CONCLUDED.

conq'ring song, We're victors, victors on the bat-tle-field, If trust-ing our King, From our hearts we can sing, The Lord is our strength and shield.

61. JESUS, SAVIOUR, PILOT ME.

Rev. EDWARD HOPPER.   J. E. GOULD.

1. Je - sus, Sav - iour, pi - lot me,   O - ver life's tempestuous sea;
2. As a moth - er stills her child,   Thou canst hush the o - cean wild;
3. When at last I near the shore,   And the fear - ful breakers roar

Unknown waves be - fore me roll,   Hid - ing rock and treach'rous shoal;
Boist'rous waves o - bey thy will,   When thou say'st to them "Be still!"
'Twixt me and the peaceful rest,   Then, while lean-ing on thy breast,

Chart and com - pass come from thee: Je - sus, Sav - iour, pi - lot me.
Wondrous Sov - 'reign of the sea, Je - sus, Sav - iour, pi - lot me.
May I hear thee say to me, "Fear not, I will pi - lot thee!"

67 COME TO THE FOUNTAIN TO-DAY.

DELIA T. WHITE. J. WESLEY EWING.

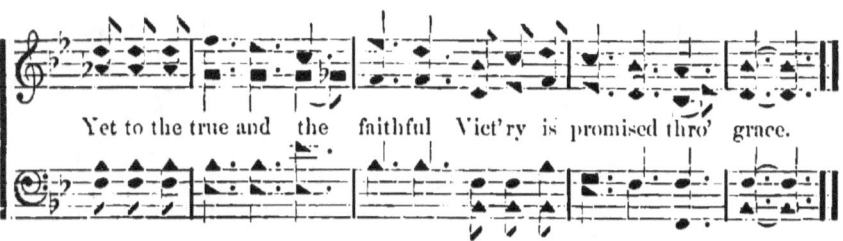

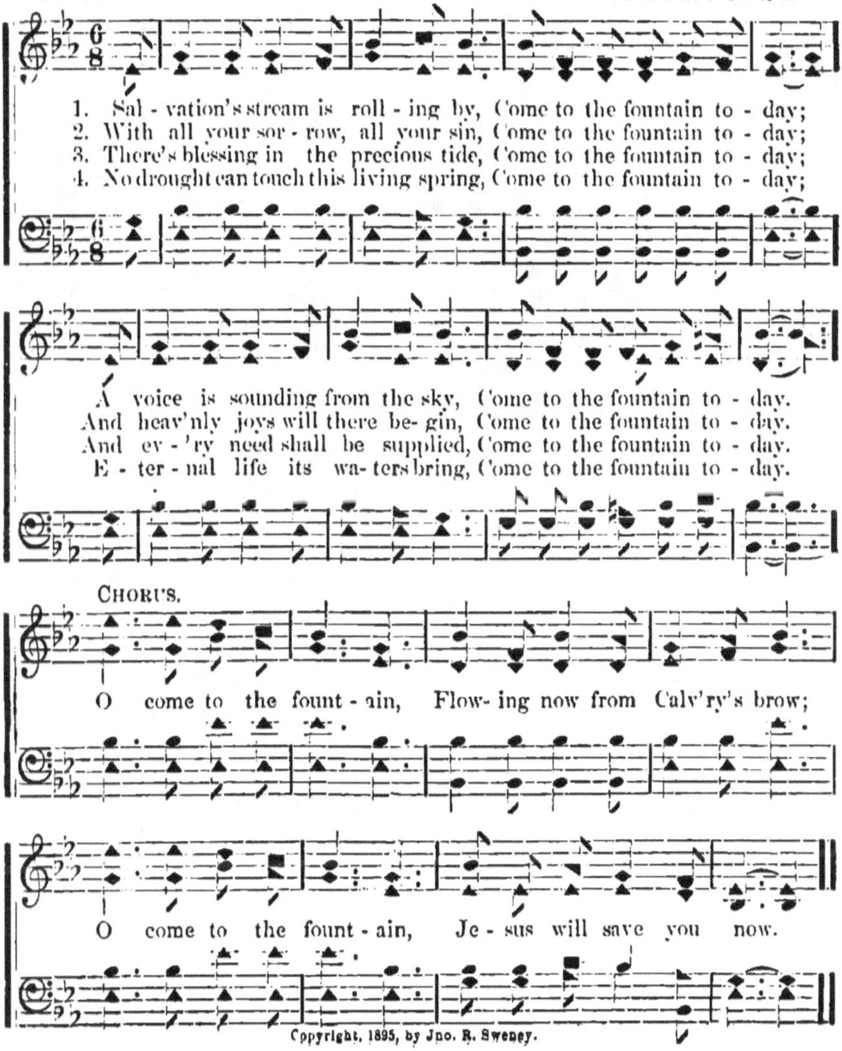

74. SALVATION'S RIVER.

R. Kelso Carter.   S. C. Foster.

1. Down at the cross, on Calvary's mountain, Where mercies flow,
    When nothing in the whole cre-a-tion Could purchase peace,
   I plunged in the re-deem-ing fount-ain, Washed whiter than the snow.
   My Saviour brought his free sal-va-tion, Gave me complete re-lease.

CHORUS.
Broth-ers, wont you hear the sto-ry? See the fount-ain flow!
Oh, glo-ry in the high-est, glo-ry! Je-sus saves me, this I know.

Copyright, 1889. John J. Hood owner.

2 When lost in sin, my all I squandered,
    Far from the fold
  My Saviour sought me where I wandered,
    Gave me his wealth untold.
  All bonds of sin and Satan rending,
    Christ made me whole,
  I'll ne'er forget that joy transcending,
    When Jesus saved my soul.

3 All round my way the sun is shining,
    Darkness has fled,
  On Jesus' breast I am reclining,
    Daily by him I'm fed.
  My Lord has cast his robe around me,
    No more I'll roam,
  The Shepherd of the sheep has found me,
    Jesus has brought me home.

E. E. Hewitt. Jno. R. Sweney.

1. O what ev-er-last-ing mer-cy Saved me, pardoned, and restored;
2. Make my life henceforth a channel, Where thy love shall have its way,
3. Free, exhaust-less is the fountain, Help me free-ly to be-lieve,

Fill me now to o-ver-flowing, With thy Ho-ly Spir-it, Lord.
Bless'd, that I may be a blessing, Use me, Saviour, ev-'ry day.
Riv-ers of thy grace are promised, More and more may I re-ceive.

Give me of the liv-ing wa-ter, Till my soul is sat-is-fied;
Clos-er, clos-er to the fountain, Hold my heart, my soul, my will;
Hap-py thirst that keeps me coming, Pleading still thy gracious word;

From the wells of thy sal-va-tion, Be my ev-'ry need sup-plied.
Let the bless-ed heav'nly currents, Rich-ly all my be-ing fill.
Fill me now to o-ver-flowing, With thy Ho-ly Spir-it, Lord.

CHORUS.

Fill me now, fill me now, To o-verflow-ing, to o-ver-
Fill me now, fill me now,

Copyright, 1897, by Jno. R. Sweney.

FILL TO OVERFLOWING.—CONCLUDED.

79 WONDERFUL PEACE.

"My peace I give unto you."—John xiv: 27.

L. H. E. L. H. EDMUNDS.

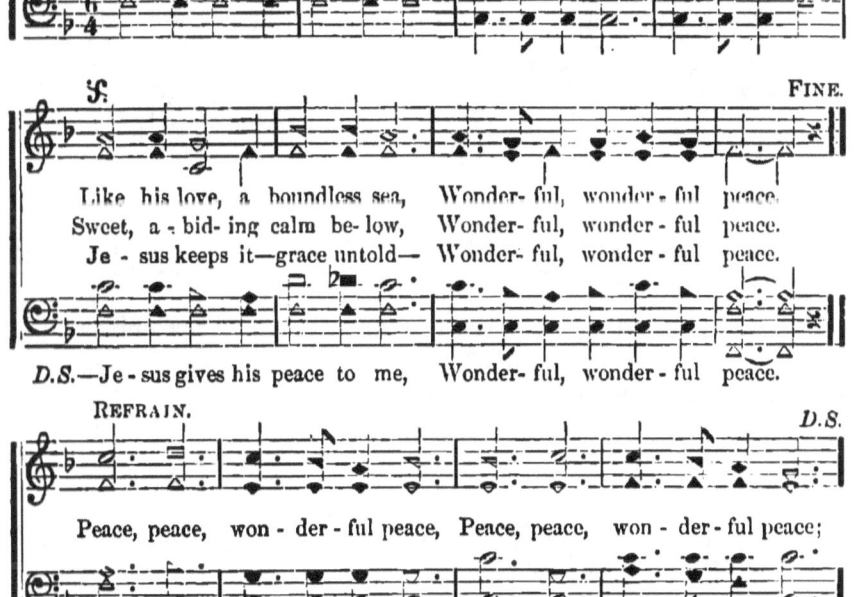

4 This my part—to trust in him,
  Wonderful peace, wonderful peace;
  Whether skies be bright or dim,
  Wonderful, wonderful peace.

5 Praying, watching, serving still,
  Wonderful peace, wonderful peace;
  Let me learn, and do his will,
  Wonderful, wonderful peace.

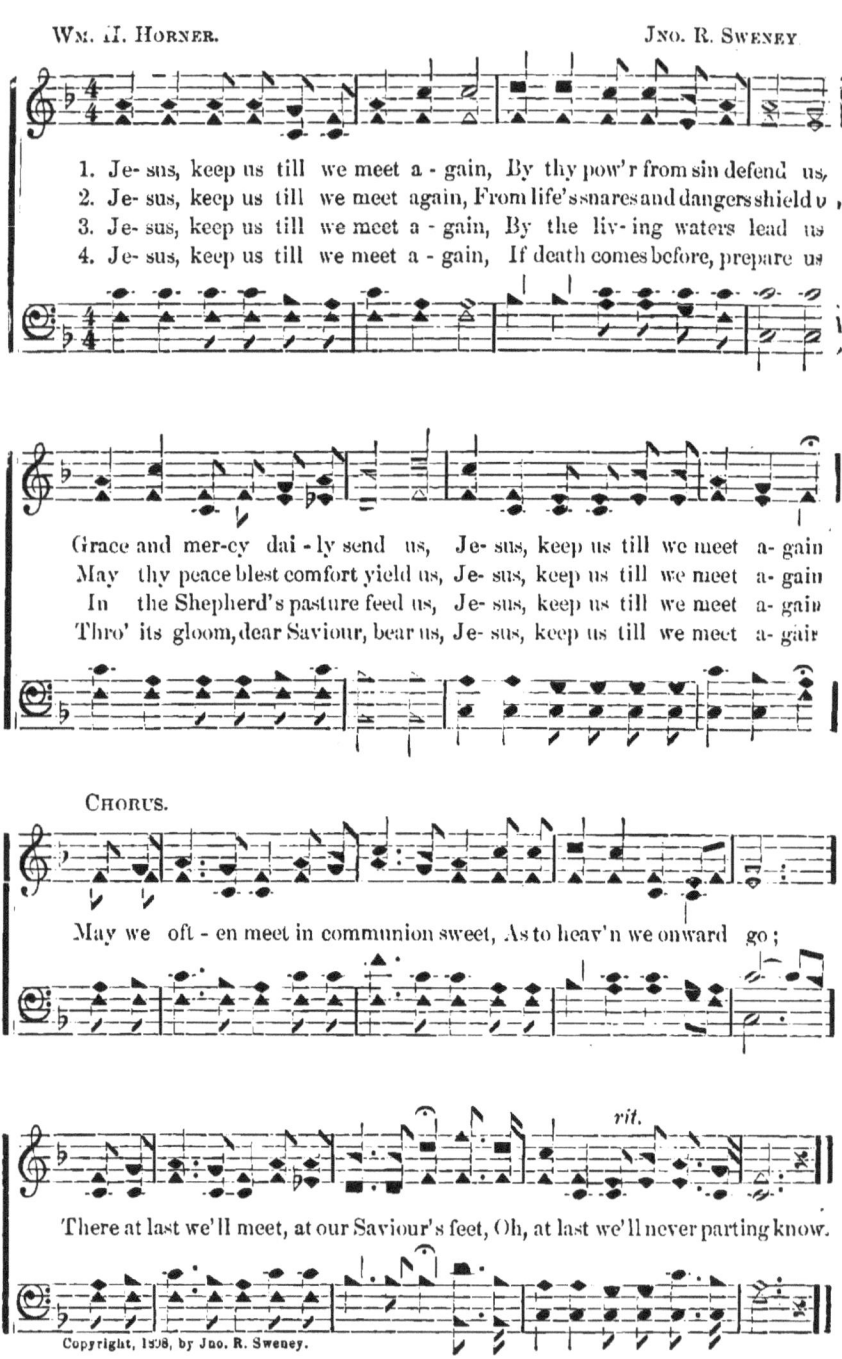

THE PENITENT'S PLEA.—CONCLUDED.

sin a-way, Pow'r to keep me sinless day by day, For me, for me!

83 ARE YOU SOWING FOR THE MASTER?

IDA L. REED.   JNO. R. SWENEY.

1. Are you sowing, dai-ly sow-ing, All a-long life's changeful way?
2. Are you sowing seeds of kindness, With a lav-ish, lov-ing hand?
3. Are you sowing, dai-ly trust-ing All the increase un - to God?

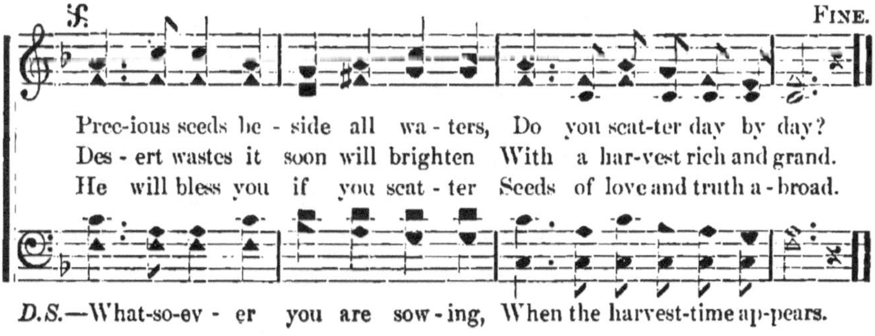

Prec-ious seeds be-side all wa-ters, Do you scat-ter day by day?
Des-ert wastes it soon will brighten With a har-vest rich and grand.
He will bless you if you scat-ter Seeds of love and truth a-broad.

D.S.—What-so-ev - er you are sow-ing, When the harvest-time ap-pears.

CHORUS.

Are you sow-ing for the Mas-ter? You shall reap in joy or tears

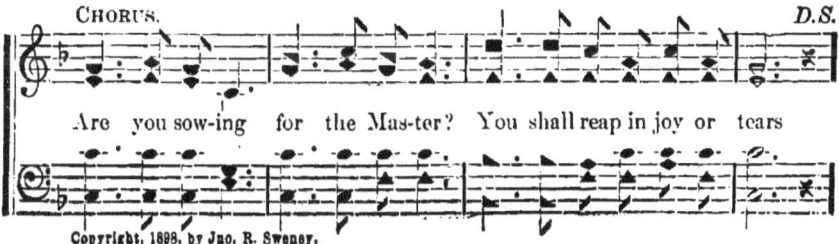

Copyright, 1898, by Jno. R. Sweney.

84. WAIT AND MURMUR NOT.

W. H. BELLAMY.   WM. J. KIRKPATRICK.

1. The home where changes never come, Nor pain nor sorrow, toil nor care;
2. Yet when bow'd down beneath the load By heav'n allow'd, thine earthly lot
3. If in thy path some thorns are found, Oh, think who bore them on his brow;
4. Toil on, nor deem, tho' sore it be, One sigh unheard, one pray'r forgot;

Yes! 'tis a bright and blessed home; Who would not fain be resting there?
Thou yearnst to reach that blest abode, Wait, meekly wait, and murmur not.
If grief thy sorrowing heart has found, It reached a ho - li - er than thou.
The day of rest will dawn for thee; Wait, meekly wait, and murmur not.

CHORUS.

O wait, (meekly wait,) meek - ly wait, and mur-mur not, O wait, (meekly wait,) meek-ly wait, and murmur not, O wait, (meekly wait,) O wait, (meekly wait,) O wait, and mur-mur not. (O murmur not.)

By permission of John J. Hood, owner of copyright.

HAMBURG. L. M.

87 While Life Prolongs.

1 While life prolongs its precious light
   Mercy is found, and peace is given,
But soon, ah! soon, approaching night
   Shall blot out every hope of heaven.

2 While God invites, how blest the day,
   How sweet the Gospel's charming sound;
Come, sinners, haste, oh, haste away,
   While yet a pardoning God is found.

3 Soon, borne on time's most rapid wing,
   Shall death command you to the grave:
Before his bar your spirits bring, [rise—
   And none be found to hear or save.

4 In that lone land of deep despair,
   No Sabbath's heavenly light shall
No God regard your bitter prayer,
   No Saviour call you to the skies.

88 Just as I am.

1 Just as I am, without one plea,
   But that thy blood was shed for me,
And that thou bids't me come to thee,
   O Lamb of God, I come! I come!

2 Just as I am, and waiting not
   To rid my soul of one dark blot, [spot,
To thee, whose blood can cleanse each
   O Lamb of God, I come! I come!

3 Just as I am, though tossed about
   With many a conflict, many a doubt,
Fightings within and fears without,
   O Lamb of God, I come! I come!

4 Just as I am—poor, wretched, blind;
   Sight, riches, healing of the mind,
Yea, all I need, in thee to find,
   O Lamb of God, I come! I come!

5 Just as I am—thou wilt receive,
   Wilt welcome, pardon, cleanse, relieve,
Because thy promise I believe,
   O Lamb of God, I come! I come!

6 Just as I am—thy love unknown
   Hath broken every barrier down;
Now, to be thine, yea, thine alone,
   O Lamb of God, I come! I come!

89 Come, Holy Spirit.

1 Come, Holy Spirit, calm my mind,
   And fit me to approach my God;
Remove each vain, each worldly thought,
   And lead me to thy blest abode.

2 Hast thou imparted to my soul
   A living spark of holy fire?
Oh! kindle now the sacred flame,
   Make me to burn with pure desire.

3 A brighter faith and hope impart,
   And let me now my Saviour see;
Oh! soothe and cheer my burdened heart,
   And bid my spirit rest in thee.

90 When I Survey.

1 When I survey the wondrous cross,
   On which the Prince of glory died,
My richest gain I count but loss,
   And pour contempt on all my pride.

2 Forbid it, Lord, that I should boast,
   Save in the death of Christ, my God;
All the vain things that charm me most,
   I sacrifice them to his blood.

3 See, from his head, his hands, his feet,
   Sorrow and love flow mingled down;
Did e'er such love and sorrow meet,
   Or thorns compose so rich a crown?

4 His dying crimson, like a robe,
   Spreads o'er his body on the tree,
Then am I dead to all the globe,
   And all the globe is dead to me.

5 Were the whole realm of nature mine,
   That were a present far too small;
Love so amazing, so divine,
   Demands my soul, my life, my all.

MISSIONARY HYMN.

L. MASON.

91. From Greenland's Icy.

1 From Greenland's icy mountains,
  From India's coral strand,
  Where Afric's sunny fountains
  Roll down their golden sand,
  From many an ancient river,
  From many a palmy plain,
  They call us to deliver
  Their land from error's chain.

2 What though the spicy breezes
  Blow soft o'er Ceylon's isle,
  Though every prospect pleases,
  And only man is vile;
  In vain with lavish kindness
  The gifts of God are strewn,
  The heathen, in their blindness,
  Bow down to wood and stone.

3 Shall we, whose souls are lighted
  With wisdom from on high,
  Shall we, to men benighted,
  The lamp of life deny?
  Salvation, oh, salvation!
  The joyful sound proclaim,
  Till earth's remotest nation
  Has learned Messiah's name.

4 Waft, waft, ye winds, his story,
  And you, ye waters, roll,
  Till, like a sea of glory,
  It spreads from pole to pole;
  Till o'er our ransomed nature,
  The Lamb for sinners slain,
  Redeemer, King, Creator,
  In bliss returns to reign.

92. Hail to the Lord's Anointed.

1 Hail to the Lord's Anointed!
  Great David's greater Son!
  Hail in the time appointed,
  His reign on earth begun!
  He comes to break oppression,
  To set the captive free,—
  To take away transgression,
  And rule in equity.

2 He shall come down like showers
  Upon the fruitful earth,
  And love and joy, like flowers,
  Spring in his path to birth:
  Before him on the mountains
  Shall peace, the herald, go;
  And righteousness, in fountains,
  From hill to valley flow.

3 For him shall prayer unceasing
  And daily vows ascend;
  His kingdom still increasing,
  A kingdom without end;
  The tide of time shall never
  His covenant remove;
  His name shall stand forever,
  That name to us is—LOVE.

93. THE MORNING LIGHT.

Samuel F. Smith.   Tune, Webb. 7, 6.

1 The morning light is breaking;
  The darkness disappears;
  The sons of earth are waking
  To penitential tears;
  Each breeze that sweeps the ocean
  Brings tidings from afar,
  Of nations in commotion,
  Prepared for Zion's war.

2 See heathen nations bending
  Before the God we love,
  And thousand hearts ascending
  In gratitude above;
  While sinners, now confessing,
  The gospel call obey,
  And seek the Saviour's blessing,
  A nation in a day.

3 Blest river of salvation,
  Pursue thine onward way:
  Flow thou to every nation,
  Nor in thy richness stay:
  Stay not till all the lowly
  Triumphant reach their home:
  Stay not till all the holy
  Proclaim, "The Lord is come!"

94. Stand up, stand up for Jesus.

Geo. Duffield, Jr.   Tune above.

1 Stand up, stand up for Jesus,
  Ye soldiers of the cross;
  Lift high his royal banner,
  It must not suffer loss;
  From victory unto victory
  His army shall he lead
  Till every foe is vanquished
  And Christ is Lord indeed.

2 Stand up, stand up for Jesus,
  The trumpet call obey;
  Forth to the mighty conflict,
  In this his glorious day:
  "Ye that are men, now serve him,"
  Against unnumbered foes:
  Your courage rise with danger,
  And strength to strength oppose.

3 Stand up, stand up for Jesus,
  Stand in his strength alone;
  The arm of flesh will fail you;
  Ye dare not trust your own:
  Put on the gospel armor,
  And watching unto prayer;
  Where duty calls, or danger,
  Be never wanting there.

4 Stand up, stand up for Jesus,
  The strife will not be long;
  This day the noise of battle,
  The next the victor's song:
  To him that overcometh,
  A crown of life shall be;
  He with the King of glory
  Shall reign eternally.

95. Work, for the Night is Coming.

1 Work, for the night is coming,
  Work through the morning hours;
  Work, while the dew is sparkling,
  Work 'mid springing flowers;
  Work, when the day grows brighter,
  Work in the glowing sun;
  Work, for the night is coming,
  When man's work is done.

2 Work, for the night is coming,
  Work through the sunny noon;
  Fill brightest hours with labor,
  Rest comes sure and soon,
  Give every flying minute
  Something to keep in store:
  Work, for the night is coming,
  When man works no more.

3 Work, for the night is coming,
  Under the sunset skies;
  While their bright tints are glowing,
  Work, for daylight flies.
  Work till the last beam fadeth,
  Fadeth to shine no more;
  Work while the night is darkening,
  When man's work is o'er.

BOYLSTON. S. M.

LOWELL MASON.

96 And can I yet Delay?

AND can I yet delay
My little all to give?
To tear my soul from earth away
For Jesus to receive?

2 Nay, but I yield, I yield;
I can hold out no more:
I sink, by dying love compelled,
And own thee conqueror.

3 Though late, I all forsake;
My friends, my all resign:
Gracious Redeemer, take, oh, take,
And seal me ever thine.

4 Come, and possess me whole,
Nor hence again remove;
Settle and fix my wavering soul
With all thy weight of love.

97 A Charge to Keep I have.

A CHARGE to keep I have,
A God to glorify;
A never-dying soul to save,
And fit it for the sky.

2 To serve the present age,
My calling to fulfill,—
Oh, may it all my powers engage
To do my Master's will.

3 Arm me with jealous care,
As in thy sight to live;
And oh, thy servant, Lord, prepare,
A strict account to give.

4 Help me to watch and pray,
And on thyself rely,
Assured, if I my trust betray,
I shall forever die.

LABAN. S. M.

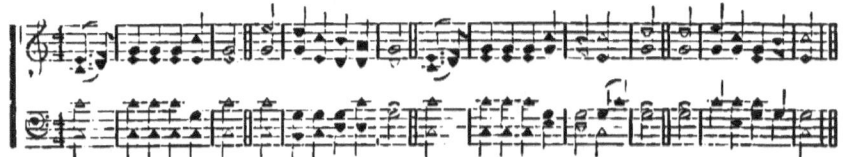

98 Come, We that Love the Lord.

COME, we that love the Lord,
And let our joys be known;
Join in a song with sweet accord,
And thus surround his throne.

2 Let those refuse to sing
Who never knew our God,
But servants of the heavenly King
May speak their joys abroad.

3 The men of grace have found
Glory begun below;
Celestial fruit on earthly ground
From faith and hope may grow:

4 Then let our songs abound,
And every tear be dry;
We're marching through Immanuel's
To fairer worlds on high. [ground,

99 My Soul, be on Thy Guard.

MY soul, be on thy guard,
Ten thousand foes arise,
And hosts of sin are pressing hard
To draw thee from the skies.

2 Oh, watch, and fight, and pray,
The battle ne'er give o'er,
Renew it boldly every day,
And help divine implore.

3 Ne'er think the victory won,
Nor once at ease sit down;
Thine arduous work will not be done
Till thou hast got the crown.

4 Fight on, my soul, till death
Shall bring thee to thy God:
He'll take thee, at thy parting breath,
Up to his blest abode.

ST. THOMAS. S. M.

100 My Soul, Repeat His Praise.

1 My soul, repeat his praise,
　Whose mercies are so great;
Whose anger is so slow to rise,
　So ready to abate.

2 High as the heavens are raised
　Above the ground we tread,
So far the riches of his grace
　Our highest thoughts exceed.

3 His power subdues our sins,
　And his forgiving love
Far as the east is from the west,
　Doth all our guilt remove.

4 The pity of the Lord,
　To those who fear his name,
Is such as tender parents feel;
　He knows our feeble frame.

101 Jesus, Who Knows Full Well.

1 Jesus, who knows full well
　The heart of every saint,
Invites us all our griefs to tell,
　To pray and never faint.

2 He bows his gracious ear,
　We never plead in vain:
Yet we must wait till he appear,
　And pray, and pray again.

3 Though unbelief suggest,
　Why should we longer wait!
He bids us never give him rest,
　But be importunate.

4 Jesus the Lord will hear
　His chosen, when they cry;
Yes, though he may awhile forbear,
　He'll help them from on high.

102 Welcome, Sweet Day of Rest.

1 Welcome, sweet day of rest,
　That saw the Lord arise,
Welcome to this reviving breast,
　And these rejoicing eyes.

2 The King himself comes near,
　And feasts his saints to-day;
Here we may sit, and see him here,
　And love, and praise, and pray.

3 One day amidst the place
　Where my dear God hath been,
Is sweeter than ten thousand days
　Of pleasureable sin.

4 My willing soul would stay
　In such a frame as this,
And sit and sing herself away
　To everlasting bliss.

103 Come, Holy Spirit, Come.

1 Come, Holy Spirit, come,
　Let thy bright beams arise;
Dispel the darkness from our minds,
　And open thou our eyes.

2 Revive our drooping faith,
　Our doubts and fears remove,
And kindle in our breasts the flame
　Of never-dying love.

3 'Tis thine to cleanse the heart,
　To sanctify the soul,
To pour fresh life on every part,
　And new create the whole.

4 Dwell, therefore, in our hearts,
　Our minds from bondage free;
Then shall we know, and praise, and love
　The Father, Son and Thee.

HORTON. 7s.

104   Come, Said Jesus.

1 Come, said Jesus' sacred voice,
Come, and make my path your choice,
I will guide you to your home;
Weary pilgrim, hither come.

2 Thou who, houseless, sole, forlorn,
Long hast borne the proud world's scorn,
Long hast roamed the barren waste,
Weary pilgrim, hither haste.

3 Ye who, tossed on beds of pain,
Seek for ease, but seek in vain;
Ye, by fiercer anguish torn,
In remorse for guilt who mourn;

4 Hither come, for here is found
Balm that flows for every wound,
Peace that ever shall endure,
Rest eternal, sacred, sure.

105   As the Twilight Shadows.

1 As the twilight shadows fall,
Let us, in the closing day,
Mark the solemn hour when all
Earthly things shall fade away.

2 In the grave to which we haste,
No repentance can be found;
Shall we then our moments waste
While we stand on trial-ground?

3 Ere the coming of that night,
(When it's coming who can say?)
Let us do with all our might,
Strive and labor, watch and pray.

4 Lord, do thou thy grace impart;
Penitence and faith bestow!
Come and sanctify each heart,
Let us thy salvation know.

5 That when waning years have fled,
And these scenes have passed away,
Rising with the summoned dead,
We may wake to endless day.

106   Gentle Jesus.

1 Gentle Jesus, meek and mild,
Look upon a little child;
Pity my simplicity,
Suffer me to come to thee.

2 Fain I would to thee be brought;
Gracious God, forbid it not;
Give me, O my God, a place
In the kingdom of thy grace!

3 Put thy hands upon my head,
Let me in thine arms be stayed;
Let me lean upon thy breast,
Lull me there, O Lord, to rest.

4 Fain I would be as thou art;
Give me thy obedient heart;
Thou art pitiful and kind;
Let me have thy loving mind.

107   Depth of Mercy!

1 Depth of mercy! can there be
Mercy still reserved for me?
Can my God his wrath forbear,—
Me, the chief of sinners, spare?

2 I have long withstood his grace;
Long provoked him to his face;
Would not hearken to his calls;
Grieved him by a thousand falls.

3 Now incline me to repent;
Let me now my sins lament;
Now my foul revolt deplore,
Weep, believe, and sin no more.

4 Kindled his relentings are;
Me he now delights to spare;
Cries, 'how can I give thee up?'
Lets the lifted thunder drop.

5 There for me the Saviour stands,
Shows his wounds, and spreads his
God is love! I know, I feel; [hands;
Jesus weeps, and loves me still.

108. The Haven of Rest. (Copyr't.)

My soul in sad exile was out on life's sea,
So burdened with sin and distrest,
Till I heard a sweet voice saying, make me your choice;
And I entered the "Haven of Rest!"

CHO.—I've anchored my soul in the haven of rest,
I'll sail the wide seas no more;
The tempest may sweep o'er the wild, stormy deep,
In Jesus I'm safe evermore.

2 I yielded myself to his tender embrace,
And faith taking hold of the word,
My fetters fell off and I anchored my soul;
The haven of rest is my Lord.

3 The song of my soul, since the Lord made me whole,
Has been the OLD STORY so blest
Of Jesus, who'll save whosoever will have
A home in the "Haven of Rest!"

4 How precious the thought that we all may recline,
Like John the beloved and blest,
On Jesus' strong arm, where no tempest can harm,—
Secure in the "Haven of Rest!"

5 Oh, come to the Saviour, he patiently waits
To save by his power divine;
Come, anchor your soul in the haven of rest,
And say, "my beloved is mine."
—H. L. Gilmour.

109. Blessed Assurance. (Copyr't.)

BLESSED assurance, Jesus is mine!
Oh, what a foretaste of glory divine!
Heir of salvation, purchase of God,
Born of his Spirit, washed in his blood.

CHO.—‖: This is my story, this is my song,
Praising my Saviour all the day long. :‖

2 Perfect submission, perfect delight,
Visions of rapture burst on my sight,
Angels descending, bring from above
Echoes of mercy, whispers of love.

3 Perfect submission, all is at rest,
I in my Saviour am happy and blest,
Watching and waiting, looking above,
Fill'd with his goodness, lost in his love.
—Fanny J. Crosby.

110. Is my Name Written There? (Cop.)

LORD, I care not for riches,
Neither silver nor gold;
I would make sure of heaven,
I would enter the fold.
In the book of thy kingdom,
With its pages so fair,
Tell me, Jesus, my Saviour,
Is my name written there?

CHO.—Is my name written there,
On the page white and fair?
In the book of thy kingdom,
Is my name written there?

2 Lord, my sins are so many,
Like the sands of the sea,
But thy blood, oh, my Saviour!
Is sufficient for me;
For thy promise is written,
In bright letters that glow,
"Though your sins be as scarlet,
I will make them like snow."

3 Oh! that beautiful city,
With its mansions of light,
With its glorified beings,
In pure garments of white;
Where no evil thing cometh,
To despoil what is fair;
Where the angels are watching—
Is my name written there?—M. A. K.

111. Lead Me, Saviour. (Copyr't.)

SAVIOUR, lead me, lest I stray,
Gently lead me all the way;
I am safe when by thy side,
I would in thy love abide.

CHO.—Lead me, lead me,
Saviour, lead me, lest I stray,
Gently down the stream of time,
Lead me, Saviour, all the way.

2 Thou the refuge of my soul
While life's stormy billows roll,
I am safe when thou art nigh,
All my hopes on thee rely.

3 Saviour, lead me, then at last,
When the storm of life is past,
To the land of endless day,
Where all tears are wiped away.
—Frank M. Davis.

112 Glory to His Name. (*Copyr't.*)

Down at the cross where my Saviour died,
Down where for cleansing from sin I
  cried;
There to my heart was the blood applied;
  Glory to his name.

Cho.—Glory to his name,
  Glory to his name;
There to my heart was the blood ap- [plied;
  Glory to his name.

2 I am so wondrously saved from sin,
Jesus so sweetly abides within;
There at the cross where he took me in;
  Glory to his name.

3 Oh, precious fountain, that saves from
I am so glad I have entered in; [sin!
There Jesus saves me and keeps me clean;
  Glory to his name.

4 Come to this fountain, so rich and sweet;
Cast thy poor soul at the Saviour's feet;
Plunge in to-day, and be made complete;
  Glory to his name.
—Rev. E. A. Hoffman.

113 The Everlasting Arms. (*Copyr't.*)

What a fellowship, what a joy divine,
  Leaning on the everlasting arms;
What a blessedness, what a peace is mine,
  Leaning on the everlasting arms.

Cho.—Leaning, leaning,
  Safe and secure from all alarms,
    Leaning, leaning,
  Leaning on the everlasting arms.

2 Oh, how sweet to walk in this pilgrim
    way,
  Leaning on the everlasting arms;
Oh, how bright the path grows from day to
    day,
  Leaning on the everlasting arms.

3 What have I to dread, what have I to
    fear,
  Leaning on the everlasting arms?
I have blessed peace with my Lord so near,
  Leaning on the everlasting arms.
—Rev. E. A. Hoffman.

114 My Jesus, I Love Thee. (*Copyr't.*)

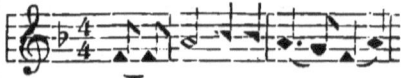

My Jesus, I love thee, I know thou art mine,
For thee all the follies of sin I resign;
My gracious Redeemer, my Saviour art thou,
If ever I loved thee, my Jesus, 'tis now.

2 I love thee because thou hast first loved me,
And purchased my pardon on Calvary's tree;
I love thee for wearing the thorns on thy brow;
If ever I loved thee, my Jesus, 'tis now.

3 I will love thee in life, I'll love thee in death,
And praise thee as long as thou lendest me
    breath;
And say, when the death-dew lies cold on
    my brow,
If ever I loved thee, my Jesus, 'tis now.

4 In mansions of glory and endless delight
I'll ever adore thee in heaven so bright,
I'll sing with the glittering crown on my brow,
If ever I loved thee, my Jesus, 'tis now.
—London Hymn Book.

115 Sunshine in the Soul. (*Copyr't*)

There's sunshine in my soul to-day,
  More glorious and bright
Than glows in any earthly sky,
  For Jesus is my light.

Cho.—Oh, there's sunshine, blessed sun-
    shine,
  When the peaceful, happy moments
    roll;
  When Jesus shows his smiling face
  There is sunshine in the soul.

2 There is music in my soul to-day,
  A carol to my King,
And Jesus, listening, can hear
  The songs I cannot sing.

3 There's springtime in my soul to-day,
  For when the Lord is near
The dove of peace sings in my heart,
  The flowers of grace appear.

4 There's gladness in my soul to-day,
  And hope, and praise, and love,
For blessings which he gives me now,
  And joys "laid up" above.
—E. E. Hewitt.

INDEX.

Titles in CAPITALS; First lines in Roman type.

	HYMN.
A charge to keep I have,	97
A hand all bruised and bleeding,	44
A LIGHT IN OUR FATHER'S HOUSE,	55
All the fields are growing whiter,	65
And can I yet delay?	96
Angels above are singing,	27
Are you happy in the Lord,	68
ARE YOU SOWING FOR THE MAS-	83
Are you sowing, daily sowing,	83
As the twilight shadows fall,	105
As we journey on our pathway,	43
Blessed assurance, Jesus is mine!	109
Blessed Bible, Book of Gold,	75
Blessed Lily of the Valley,	72
Come, contrite one, and seek his	23
Come, Holy Spirit, calm my mind,	89
Come, Holy Spirit, come,	103
Come in, come in, O blessed One,	26
COME IN, O BLESSED ONE,	26
Come, said Jesus' sacred voice,	104
COME TO THE FOUNTAIN TO-DAY,	67
Come to the Saviour, believe in	51
Come, ye that love the Lord,	98
Conquering now and still to con-	66
CROSSING ONE BY ONE,	20
Depth of mercy, can there be	107
DON'T YOU KNOW HE CARES?	37
Dost thou know at thy bolted	8
Down at the cross, on Calvary's	74
Down at the cross, where my Sav-	112
FILL TO OVERFLOWING,	78
From Greenland's icy mountains,	91
Gentle Jesus, meek and mild,	106
GLORIOUS VICTORY,	30
GLORY TO HIS NAME,	112
Go forth at Christ's command,	18
Hail to the Lord's anointed!	92
HALLOW HIS NAME WITH SONG,	63
HEAR THE MASTER'S CALL,	65
HE IS MINE, I AM HIS,	72
HE IS PRECIOUS,	42
HIGHER GROUND,	35

	HYMN.
I'LL GO WHERE YOU WANT ME TO	36
I'LL NOT BE A STRANGER UP	64
I LOVE HIM FAR BETTER,	39
I love the mercy seat,	73
I'm pressing on the upward way,	35
I must have the Saviour with me,	76
IN THAT CITY,	69
In the fight against sin,	50
In the rosy morning hours,	58
In the shelter of the Saviour's love,	32
INTO HIS MARVELLOUS LIGHT,	13
IS IT NOTHING TO YOU?.	41
IS MY NAME WRITTEN THERE?	110
It may not be on the mountain's	36
It pays to serve Jesus, I speak	39
I've been a wand'rer far from G..	10
I WILL SAY "YES" TO JESUS,	10
Jesus gives his peace to me,	79
JESUS GUIDES ME ALL THE WAY,	1
JESUS IS ALL THAT YOU NEED,	51
Jesus is my joy and sunshine,	16
JESUS IS PASSING BY,	23
Jesus is the Altogether Lovely,	2
Jesus is the light, the way,	34
Jesus, keep us till we meet again,	80
JESUS LEADS,	3
Jesus, Saviour, pilot me.	61
JESUS WILL GIVE YOU REST,	85
Jesus, who knows full well,	101
JOIN, YE SONS OF MEN,	2
JOURNEY IN THE KING'S HIGH-	12
JOY AND SUNSHINE,	16
Just as I am, without one plea,	88
Just one touch as he moves along,	71
KEEP US TILL WE MEET AGAIN,	80
LEAD ME, SAVIOUR,	111
LEANING ON THE EVERLASTING	113
LEND A HAND,	24
LET CHRIST COME IN,	38
Let us be triumphant Christians,	81
Life wears a different face to me,	86
LIKE AN ARMY STRONG,	6
Like a shepherd, tender, true,	3
List to the story,	9

Living for Jesus meekly each day,	59
LIVING FOR JESUS ONLY.	59
Lord, I care not for riches,	110
Lost, lost on the mountains of sin	54
LOYALTY TO CHRIST,	18
Many souls are sinking in the	24
March on, happy soldiers, rejoice	60
More about Jesus would I know,	5
My Jesus, I love thee, I know	114
MY SAVIOUR FIRST OF ALL,	19
My soul, be on thy guard,	99
My soul in sad exile was out on	108
My soul, repeat his praise,	100
My soul, stay not in shadows,	21
Nearer, my God, to thee!	25
NEVER SAY "NO" TO JESUS,	50
No danger can my soul affright,	17
Nothing is too hard for Jesus,	22
O'er death's sea, in yon blest city,	69
OH, DON'T YOU HEAR HIM KNOCK-	44
Oh, the joy that we may know	47
Oh, to have the mind of Jesus,	46
O idler, why loiter the bright	40
O Lord, thy mighty grace impart,	38
One sweet hour alone with Jesus,	29
On for Jesus! steady be your	49
ON TO VICTORY.	53
Our blessed Redeemer is passing	41
OUR STRENGTH AND SHIELD,	60
OUT BEYOND THE BREAKERS,	45
Out of shadow into light,	1
O what everlasting mercy,	78
O WHY STAND YE IDLE?	40
Prayer is the key,	11
REDEEMED THRO' THE BLOOD,	32
Rejoice, O children of God,	63
RESTING AT THE CROSS,	28
SALVATION'S RIVER,	74
Salvation's stream is rolling,	67
Saviour, hear me, while before	82
Saviour, lead me, lest I stray,	111
Send out the searchlight in sin's	14
Send out the sunlight, the sun-	48
SEND THE FIRE JUST NOW,	4
SHALL I TURN BACK?	54
SINCE CHRIST THE LORD IS MINE,	17
SINCE I FOUND MY SAVIOUR,	86
SINGING AS WE GO,	70
Standing on the promises of Christ	63
Stand up, stand up for Jesus,	94
STEP BY STEP,	31

SUNSHINE IN THE SOUL,	115
TELL IT OUT WITH GLADNESS,	68
THE BEAUTIFUL LIGHT,	34
THE CALL TO ARMS,	15
THE CROSS IS NOT GREATER,	77
The cross that he gave may be	77
THE GOLDEN KEY,	11
THE HAPPY SONG,	47
THE HARBOR HOME,	52
THE HAVEN OF REST,	108
The home where changes never	84
THE KNOCK OF THE NAIL-PIERCED	8
THE LIFE ON WINGS,	21
THE MIND OF JESUS,	46
The morning light is breaking,	93
THE PENITENT'S PLEA,	82
There is a danger line on the sea	45
There's a beautiful homeland by	64
There's a call for soldiers on the	15
There's sunshine in my soul to-	115
THE SAVIOUR WITH ME,	76
THE SUNNY SIDE OF THE CROSS,	81
Tho' your sins be as scarlet,	56
To the cross of Christ,	28
VICTORY THROUGH GRACE,	66
Victory, victory, glorious victory,	80
WAIT, AND MURMUR NOT,	84
WASH ME IN THY BLOOD,	33
We are building on the Rock, the	7
We are marching on like an army	6
We are on the winning side,	57
Welcome, sweet day of rest,	102
WE PASS THIS WAY BUT ONCE,	43
We're marching to a land of joy.	70
We shall cross the mystic river	20
What a fellowship, what a joy	113
When I survey the wondrous cross,	90
When my life work is ended, and	19
When the heart, made pure, is	42
When your spirit bows in sorrow,	37
Where'er he leads us we can go,	31
Wheresoe'er we be on life's raging	55
While life prolongs its precious	87
While we now, dear Lord, at thy	4
Will you come, will you come	85
Wonderful mercy that sought us,	13
WONDERFUL PEACE,	79
WORK FOR JESUS,	58
Work for the night is coming,	95
Would you go rejoicing on,	12
Would you to your Saviour now be	38
You're sailing t'ward the fearful	52

www.ingramcontent.com/pod-product-compliance
Lightning Source LLC
Chambersburg PA
CBHW020933180426
43192CB00036B/1035